THE
ASTROPASTORALS

THE
ASTROPASTORALS

Douglas Crase

PRESSED WAFER

Cover portrait of the author: TREVOR WINKFIELD

Design & Typesetting: JONATHAN GREENE

ISBN 978-1-940396-28-6

FIRST EDITION
Printed in the United States of America

PRESSED WAFER
375 Parkside Avenue, Brooklyn, NY 11226
www.pressedwafer.com

Contents

Once the Sole Province   1

A reductionism that makes the world   3

Dog Star Sale   4

Sale II   6

Theme Park   7

True Solar Holiday   8

Under the rim of maybe   10

To the Light Fantastic   11

Connecticut   13

The pays d'en haut Sublime   14

Astropastoral   15

Time: when not to come undone   17

Refuge   18

Once the Sole Province

                                        of genius here at home,
Was it this, our idea of access to a larger world
That invented the world itself (first, second,
Third), past accuracy we are bound to inhabit now
As targets, positioned in a trillionth
Of the smallest measuring—microresults
Made in the least, most unimaginable chronology?
No more time-outs. For we are either ready or
We must be ready or not, an expensive mix
Of life-based chemistry perpetually on the verge
Of going to heaven in a vapor, and almost making it,
Almost, except there's that one true destiny
Incontestably driving down on us,
The finally collapsible ones,
Who are lumped in a uniform density at last,
At last coherent to desire. It is a density
Greater than the sun's.

                                        But Day,
There must be some other reference,
Which is why you so nervously dwell on us,
On earth which keeps turning, embarrassed, from the light:
Indiscriminate shine on Shiite, Methodist, Hun,
And pump of excitability. Dissatisfied,
As all things are on earth,
Is there anything earthly that can't be made to rise,
Emit disciples, the collimated and the laser lean?
They march to you, old outside agitator,
While you who pump the world with promises

I

Are simply not to be believed. All those diversions,
The years and decades, the manifold span of life
—These were the dialectic of a fold
Formed out of almost nothingness, a fold of hours
In a space where the 'hour' is eccentricity. So
Pity the day, beyond which we can see,
For if time is distance then distance must be life
And who is there on earth who will not go
In answer to its call? Call this
The aim of every reverence:
That outside ourselves there be a scale more vast,
Time free of whimsy, an endless unbended reach
In which to recollect our planet, our hours, and ourselves.

A reductionism that makes the world
complex, a truth that simply nothing
can explain, is how events curled
up in space when seen are scattering.

Dog Star Sale

Now the universe wants to be known
For itself, isn't that why we're here
Popped out on this terrace the color of stars
The red ones like gentrified brick

Lucky for us
It takes money to even imagine
Such things and this, for parsecs around,
Is the one place where money is made
Though not everyone has it, not even here

The burden is on those who do
Which we freely take up
A volitional duty to curate the spheres
After how many misfired suns
And misapplied genes
How many millions fed to despair
Before we were brought to the task
Thankless, that cannot be failed

Just to think of it
Sometimes engenders a chill
So thorough the planet's own breath
Will draw back on its bones
And there in that vault sucked by fear
One has shivered at twinkles of something
Not normally shown

It explains the wide pupils
And why I protect them
When doing so keeps me from you
All involved on the earth with your chores of pollution
And likely never to pause
Let alone practice what we
Observe: as far as you touch
Other worlds, that much you save yours

Sale II

So the promotionals
Get harder to resist this way
And ditto the things
They advertise. All could be mine
Just for ditching this live indecision
Some tend to call
As if they knew what to compare it to
Life on the earth

Let them not count me out
Let me read their desires to ignition
And then let me burn
Intensely as they burn
In faith like a prairie fire. Don't
Let me retire too soon from the mission
To light out for anywhere just as we are
To settle our plan for salvation
On the first spinning rock of the first
Rock-surrounded dim star. O pilgrims
And real-estate shock troops
Look who's for hire

Theme Park

Too much of a subject can interfere,
Be a drag, so subvert the procedure to which it refers
That the wisest course is to visit it just for fun,
Have fun, and make a clean getaway—wisdom
Already shed in the shiver of pilgrim foot
On the longed-for soil. Truly no one ahead,
Until this is where our lives become sweet and true,
Begun on the clumpy green with its circle of flowers,
Its flagpole and founders' memorial, map
Of self-guided tours, viewing sites, trail.
And farther, more deeply recessed and peacefuller
Still, the substantive structures themselves
Are seen meeting their needs in scale: shops,
Ammo dumps, taverns, and houses of prayer. But
Who could be sure of a tenure except in this world,
Fair between the river and the sea?—where the birds
And the natives, so enthused by our coming,
Run back and forth like children on the shore.

True Solar Holiday

Out of the whim of data,
Out of binary contests driven and stored,
By the law of large numbers and subject to that law
Which in time will correct us like an event,
And from bounce and toss of things that aren't even things
I've determined the trend I call 'you' and know you are real,
Your unwillingness to appear
In all but the least likely worlds, as in this world
Here. In spite of excursions, despite my expenditures
Ever more anxiously matrixed, ever baroque,
I can prove we have met and I've proved we can do it again
By each error I make where otherwise one couldn't be
Because only an actual randomness
Never admits a mistake. It's for your sake,
Then, *though the stars get lost from the bottle,*
Though the bottle unwind, if I linger around in the wrong
Ringing up details, pixel by high bit by bit,
In hopes of you not as integer but at least as the sum
Of all my near misses, divisible
Once there is time to an average that poses you perfectly
Like a surprise, unaccidentally credible
Perfectly like a surprise. Am I really too patient,
When this is the only program from which you derive?
Not if you knew how beautiful you will be,
How important it is your discovery dawn on me,
How as long as I keep my attention trained
Then finally the days
Will bow every morning in your direction as they do to the sun

That hosannas upon that horizon
Of which I am witness and not the one farther on
—Set to let me elect you as though there were no other choice,
Choice made like temperature, trend I can actually feel.

Under the rim of maybe
Back on the edge of regret
Around the corner from should have
Down the street from forget
Out on a limb with willing
Too far gone to remark
Close to the tip of almost
Up slip creek in the dark

To the Light Fantastic

Nor are the fashions always fickle
Or imposed, but may occur as breakthroughs
In tandem with our need for them, the need
They were orbiting unnoticed all that time.
Invented, these burst upon a world agog
With its own gravity, a world of matter
Where the trade is energy, a world
Whose minds in many private laboratories
May suddenly wave an identical flag
In each of them, the report of which
Thrills all the media: a century
Begins—begins because it discovered

The rights of man, or unearthed light.
And ours? if it isn't breaking on the scene,
Must be begun somewhere in prototype,
Be protected by patents, nourished
In the flush of R & D. Somewhere,
Already in line with theory, where
The deracinated secrets reel by,
Where the cameras gaze on their unlikely provenance...

All the satellites scattered in heaven
Nod, until by laws of motion
That consortium is stirred whose teams
Reciprocate their codes from many
Terminals, knowing, the moment more
Come online than ever before, inertia
· Is undone: enlightenment—does it

Enter as light with the speed of light
To delineate all this earth (emirate,
Nation, principality) whose arrangement
Is finally making its debut, got up
In a possible planet, as was made?

Connecticut

So much motion is love.
Though sometimes it's also exile
Or the 'bent of our spirits to remove'
Nearer their venue of desire, still motion
Is love, pressed forward in hopes of
Never being left behind and never having, meanwhile,
Gone too far: a dilemma
Terribly settled here first by those, outdistanced
Otherwise, who dispelled all else before them,
Naming it New World. Fierce state of

Forgetfulness!—if ever your ancient affections
Offer a fight, if writ or rebellion
Restore them to power or redress of letters

Jimmy them free, then let me recall but one
Mere rebel more whose love you might move on to be.

The pays d'en haut Sublime

for Brian Walker

The fables were always upcountry, but
The sublime
Understood in its practical sense as
This map of vista and refuge that slides into mind
Whenever you simply are looking
Has to be here: its precincts
So free of protection, freely desired,
And reached by that hard-driving warpath
Where each vote was personal, something you feel,
Cut time. The fashions
Are always downriver, not the sublime.
It lingers the unlicensed wealth
Due to any inhabitant, some,
Who could hurry its data into an ardent shape
As if life were a sensate
Cartography. So it would seem
In this land where the maps all lie flat
Until, trying one on,
You proceed via graphic new molt as your whole country
Walking—in whose indefensible habits
Let me come too, though the facts
Turn to fables themselves, strike back and run.

Astropastoral

As much as the image of you, I have seen
You again, live, as in live indecision you brighten
The limbs of an earth that so earnestly turns
To reflect you, the sky's brightest body
And last best beacon for those who are everywhere
Coded in spirals and want to unbend,
Who bear in the dark turned toward you
This message they have to deliver even to live,
To linger in real time before you, to meet or to
Blow you away—and yes I have seen you receive them
But you are not there. Though I've tried to ignore you,
Go solo, light out beyond you,
I have seen you on every horizon, how you are stored
And encouraged and brought to the brim
Until the round bounds of one planet could not hold you in
But were ready to set near space ringing
As if from the ranking capacitor outside the sun.
I have seen you discharged, and then how you swell
Toward heaven and how you return, transmitting the fun
Of the firmament, all of it yours. And these things
Have happened, only you are not there.
At night in the opposite high-rise I'd see how you glow,
And in the adjacent one too, the same would-be blue,
And I've looked on the glow in the waters
Around the reactor, that also blue, how
Whatever would match your expression you
Wouldn't be there. I have seen the impressions you leave
At the margin of error in exit polls, monitored polls
That you never entered—I can tell what I see:

Saw you vote with your feet and hit the ground running,
Kiss the ground, rescued, and (*this wasn't a drill*)
Saw you fall to your knees on the ground
By the body of your friend on the ground
And though these fall beside you like gantries, it is
You who are rising above them and you are not there.
Like a rocket in winter, I have been there to see you
Logged in as a guest among stars—only you,
Though you're lovely to look at, expensive to own,
And though in demand without letup, you are not there.

Time: when not to come undone
is, no, not slavery. Happiness
defines the accommodation
that hides the quark from us.

Refuge

The mitigation remembers the mischief,
And nothing's repaired except to engender it
Different. All things are wild
In the service of objects toward which they verge
—Each amendment is wild, and the touch
On the refuse truck wheel tears up Valley Brook
Road. We were here for the view, and in that
We are a success because this is our scene:
Tracks, turnpike, a pipeline, the landfill,
Amenities meant for the wildlife in
The error-prone acreage between. No habitat
Scans like a wasteland, but by what unmistakable
Eye? The truck stirs the mice, the hawk
Heart stirs, and rodents in motion resolve
In fast-focus foveae. Life lifts from, it
Harries the ground, and the study a species
Must turn to is that earth
Where the dump and the refuge are relations under the sun.

The poems in this chapbook were first published separately. The earliest, 'Once the Sole Province,' appeared in 1979, was reprinted in *Ecstatic Occasions, Expedient Forms*, and translated into Italian for *Spazio Umano* in Milan. 'True Solar Holiday' was likewise translated into Italian; it appeared originally in the United Kingdom, was reprinted in *The Best of the Best American Poetry*, and inspired the electro-acoustical composition 'True Holiday,' written and performed by the Berlin-based group The Magic I.D. with lyrics written and sung by Margareth Kammerer. The last to appear, 'Astropastoral,' was published in 2000 and reprinted in the *Oxford Book of American Poetry*. The poems are collected here for the first time.

DOUGLAS CRASE is a member of the Planetary Society and the Society of the Descendants of the Founders of Hartford.